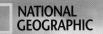

Ladders

LIVING ON THE COAST

Communities We Live In

Surf's UP

by Debbie Nevins

You are standing barefoot in the sand on a beach. The Pacific Ocean curls and crashes toward you in great, rolling waves, one after the other. You feel the salty spray on your face as the cold water tickles your feet. On the top, or **crest,** of the next big wave, you see two surfers riding on one surfboard. Whoa, that's tricky. But wait . . . one of the surfers has four legs. It's a dog!

The place where people live affects where they work, the kinds of homes they live in, and even what they do to have fun. In coastal communities, most people spend their free time on the beach. Some beaches are even dog-friendly, which means that happy pups—and their people—can relax in the sun or play in the water. Many dogs love the beach as much as people do.

Surf dog Jedi catches a wave on a California beach.

There are beachy scents to sniff, sticks to catch, birds to chase, and strangers to greet. And for some lucky dogs, especially those in southern California, there are waves to surf! Some of those four-footed **athletes** take part in surfing competitions. No wonder there are so many wet dogs and cheering people on the beaches of California!

Making a Splash

Each year, more than 1,500 pet owners and fans gather in Huntington Beach in California for the Surf City Surf Dog Competition. Doggy athletes, called "surFURS," sniff out the competition. They greet each other with tail wags and sloppy licks. Then they hop on their boards and "catch a wave." This is an unusual sports competition, but it sure is fun to watch.

Many dogs like to surf, but what about the pups on this beach that would rather stay dry? They can bark for their favorite surfers or compete in a doggy fashion show or a costume contest. Their owners can even shop for the latest in dog toys. All this cuteness is for a good cause. Some of the money raised at this community event goes to dog rescue **charities**, or groups that help others. Rescue charities find good homes for dogs that need them. In fact, many of the "surFURS" lived in shelters until rescue groups placed them into good homes.

< Check out this pup's colorful life jacket. All athletes must wear safety gear to compete.

This dog's name is Code Four. He's dressed up for the costume contest. He won first place in 2010.

Every sport has its heroes. That includes surfing. Buddy is a Jack Russell terrier. He's a famous dog surfer. He's the first dog to be honored by the Surf Dog Hall of Fame.

This dog wears goggles and a bandanna. The goggles keep salt water out of his eyes. The bandanna just makes him look cool.

Surprising SurFURS

Think surfing dogs are surprising? How about a surfing pig? Or a goat? Just about any pet can be taught to surf as long as it likes the water and can swim. Even cats can learn to surf if they don't hate the water.

Ready for Action

There's a lot to do before the Huntington Beach competition. The owners must double-check their surFURS' gear. The dogs wear floating jackets to stay safe in the deep water. Some owners wear floating jackets, too. They also practice surfing with their dogs.

When the competition begins, owners wade out with their dogs and surfboards to where the waves are just right. Then they help their pooches onto the boards and point them toward shore. When the water rises, they let go, and . . . cowabunga! Some pups ride the boards all the way to shore. Others jump off, slipping into the surf. Don't worry. Their owners are right there to help them.

To give each dog a score, judges award points for length of ride and height of wave. Standing on all fours is worth five points, sitting earns three, and lying on the board is awarded two points. Dogs earn extra points for special tricks, such as riding backwards.

∧ Surfer kitty Nicolasa rides the waves in Peru, South America.

∧ Pisco is an alpaca. Alpacas are relatives of camels. He and his owner surf in South America.

From Leashes to **Longboards**

Surfer dogs are awesome, but some people might wonder how owners train their dogs to stay upright on a board and surf a wave.

∧ SurFURS Nani, Ricochet, Dozer, and Toby ride the waves in sunny California.

NANI (Akamai Nani Nui)

Nickname: Little Bear

Breed: Bernese mountain dog

Loves: Surfing, swimming, sleeping, and eating

Favorite food: Cheese

Sample honor: Cover girl for the 2010 Surf Dog Calendar

Fun fact: Nani surfed in the movie *Marmaduke* (2009).

RICOCHET

Nickname: Rip Curl Ricki

Breed: Golden retriever

Loves: Surfing with disabled surfers, dock diving, swimming, rolling in stinky stuff, and chasing critters

Favorite food: All foods are her favorites.

Sample honor: 2010 *USA Today* Dog Hero

Fun fact: Ricochet helps disabled children learn to surf.

Most dogs start surfing by learning to be comfortable on a longboard, which is another name for a surfboard. Some owners bring a board into the house and offer their pup treats just for sitting on it. Gradually, the dog learns to balance on the wobbly board, and then it's off to the beach to try some gentle surfing. Some doggies take to it right away. Others might need more practice, but they all enjoy the fun, friendship, and exercise.

DOZER

Nickname: Da Bull 2

Breed: English bulldog

Loves: Surfing, eating, sleeping, dreaming, snoring, and soccer

Favorite food: Everything!

Sample honor: First place, Purina Incredible Dog Challenge Surf Dog Competition, 2011

Fun fact: Dozer appeared in a TV commercial for dog food.

TOBY

Breed: Shih tzu mix

Loves: Surfing, chasing cats and other small critters

Favorite food: Stuffed lamb

Sample honor: First place, small dog category, Surf City Surf Dog Competition in 2010

Fun fact: Toby's owner rescued him as a scruffy stray in an animal shelter.

Check In How do dogs learn to surf?

Welcome to the
OUTER BANKS

by Jennifer A. Smith

Welcome to the Outer Banks! The Outer Banks are a group of little islands off the coast of North Carolina. They're called **barrier islands** because they block the coastline from storms in the Atlantic Ocean. These islands are separated from North Carolina's **mainland** by a wide stretch of water called a **sound**.

Many small coastal communities are part of the Outer Banks. Kids go to school, adults go to work, and people have a lot of fun together living by the water. But it can also be tricky to live on the coast, especially during storm season.

> The Outer Banks are more than 175 miles long.

You can see on the map that the islands of the Outer Banks are long, narrow, and mostly flat. When the weather is good, it's really fun for the people who live there to play outside. But because the islands are barrier islands, they can get hit by strong storms called hurricanes. Look out! Powerful winds and waves move the sand along the coast farther inland or carry it out to the ocean. These storms can change the coasts of the island, or even cut an island in half.

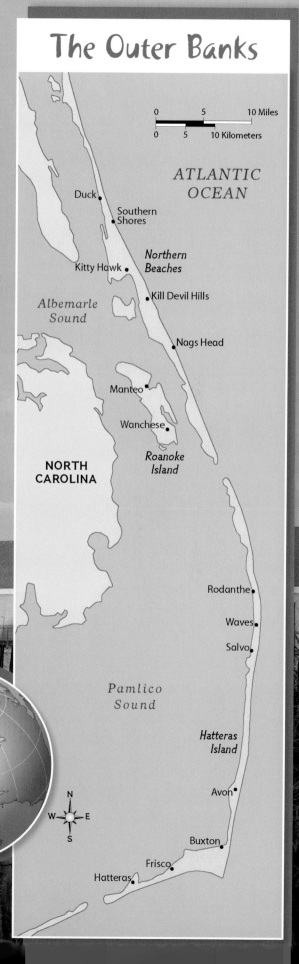

The Outer Banks

0   5   10 Miles
0   5   10 Kilometers

ATLANTIC OCEAN

Duck
Southern Shores
Northern Beaches
Kitty Hawk
Kill Devil Hills
Albemarle Sound
Nags Head
Manteo
Wanchese
Roanoke Island
NORTH CAROLINA
Rodanthe
Waves
Salvo
Pamlico Sound
Hatteras Island
Avon
Buxton
Frisco
Hatteras

N
W   E
S

First in Flight!

Kitty Hawk, North Carolina, is an Outer Banks community. It has steady winds and tall hills of sand, called dunes. In 1900, brothers Orville and Wilbur Wright were looking for a place to test an invention they called the Wright glider. A glider is an aircraft without an engine. It flies on the wind. They chose Kitty Hawk for its weather, land, and location.

The Wright brothers could glide off the high sand dunes. They could land in the soft sand. They practiced at Kitty Hawk. Then they moved to another Outer Banks community called Kill Devil Hills. There, the brothers tested gliders many times between 1901 and 1903.

> These statues are part of the Wright Brothers National Memorial. It is in Kill Devil Hills.

When they got bored with gliders, the Wrights began working on their first engine-powered airplane. In 1903, the brothers made the first successful powered flight in history. Five local citizens watched as Orville and Wilbur each took two short flights. You can check out the Wright Brothers National **Memorial** in Kill Devil Hills to learn more about the Wright brothers' first flight.

Fun on the Outer Banks

People who live on the Outer Banks in North Carolina love to have visitors. Tourists are welcome to relax on the beach and watch the waves come in. Or they can have fun doing the activities each coastal community has to offer. Take a look at some of the fun you can have in the coastal communities of the Outer Banks.

> Stunt Kite Competition, Kill Devil Hills

Go fly a kite! The long, windy beaches and sandy dunes make this the perfect place for kite flying. Outer Banks communities hold many kite-flying events during the year. These kites are competing in the Outer Banks Stunt Kite Competition.

< Lighthouse Tour, Cape Hatteras

Cape Hatteras Lighthouse is the tallest lighthouse in North America. You have to climb more than 250 steps to get to the top. It may look like the lighthouse is right on the beach in this picture, but it is actually 1,500 feet from the shore.

∧ Hang Gliding, Nags Head

Hang gliders are aircrafts that look like large kites. People strap themselves in and use the wind to soar over the ocean. You can hang glide at Jockey's Ridge State Park in Nags Head. The park has the tallest natural sand dunes on the East Coast.

∧ Sand Sculpture Festival, Nags Head

Have you ever made a sand castle? Beachgoers in Nags Head can build castles and just about anything they can think of at this sandy festival. They just grab a shovel and get to work.

Check In What is it like to live on the Outer Banks?

GENRE Comparison Article

Read to find out about the similarities and differences between two coastal communities.

Two Cities, TWO BAYS

by Brett Gover

People live in many different coastal communities around the world. Let's compare two of them to see how they are alike and different.

San Francisco, California

Along the Pacific Coast in northern California lies San Francisco Bay. Huge ships travel in and out of its deep waters. Ships must pay attention to the flow of water, or **current**, in the bay. These currents are strong and often change direction.

Next to the bay is the city of San Francisco, California, which sits on a **peninsula**, land that

∧ A cable car climbs a steep hill in San Francisco.

The Golden Gate Bridge links San Francisco with the hills of Marin County, California.

In Reykjavík, Iceland, you are never far from water.

is surrounded on three sides by water. Warm ocean air makes winters here mild and rainy, while summers are cool and foggy.

Reykjavík, Iceland

You can't get much farther north in the world than the island country of Iceland. Reykjavík (RAKE-yah-veek) is Iceland's capital.

A fishing boat floats in Reykjavík harbor.

Like San Francisco, Reykjavík sits on a peninsula along a large bay. Because it is in *Ice*land, you might expect Reykjavík to be bitterly cold. In fact, ocean currents bring warm water and mild air to Iceland's shores. This keeps the weather very pleasant.

This boy is panning for gold in the mountains near San Francisco. People have searched for gold here for more than 150 years.

San Francisco Resources

In 1769, Spanish explorers built a little town called Yerba Buena. That town was renamed San Francisco in 1847. Soon after the town changed its name, many people traveled there to search for treasure.

Have you ever heard of the California Gold Rush? In the 1840s, people found gold in the streams of the California mountains. Many excited miners traveled to the area hoping to find more gold and to get rich. Other people went to open hotels and stores for the miners and their families. San Francisco soon became a booming city.

Reykjavík Resources

People known as the *Norse* traveled to Iceland 1,100 years ago because of the plentiful fish and the good soil. They named their settlement Reykjavík, which means "Bay of Smoke." The name came from the steam they saw rising up from the ground. When the Norse looked for a reason for the steam, they found hot springs underneath the town.

Many years later, fishing and raising sheep for **wool** became the leading ways for the people of Reykjavík to earn money. Wool is soft, curly sheep's hair. It can be made into warm blankets and sweaters. Selling wool and fish to other areas turned this small village into Iceland's largest and most important city.

∧ Sheep farms are all over the island of Iceland.

Food in San Francisco

Have you ever eaten sourdough bread? Its sour taste was popular with gold miners. They liked it so much they became known as "Sourdoughs." Bakeries still make the bread fresh every day in San Francisco.

If sourdough bread doesn't sound good to you, maybe something sweeter will—like chocolate! In 1849, Domingo Ghirardelli (gir-ahr-DELL-ee) heard about the California Gold Rush and traveled there from Italy to find gold. He didn't find any. Instead, he built a chocolate factory in the city. Today, Ghirardelli chocolate is eaten all around the world.

This San Francisco baker shapes the sourdough into loaves. Then he bakes it in the oven. It will turn golden brown.

▽ This fisherman unloads a box of codfish. He is on a ship in Reykjavík harbor.

Food in Reykjavík

If you ever visit Reykjavík, you'd better like seafood! Fish and seafood are very popular there. Fishermen pull salmon, herring, and cod fresh from the ocean all year.

People in Reykjavík like to eat sweets, too, just as in San Francisco. Candy shopping there is extra fun on the weekends. Every Saturday, most candy stores sell their sweet treats for half the price!

San Francisco Sights

It's easy to have fun in San Francisco. Hop onto a cable car and ride it to the top of Lombard Street. Enjoy an exciting walk, zigzagging down this steep and curving street. By the time you get to the bottom, you'll be very hungry.

Make your way to a Chinatown restaurant for a yummy bowl of noodles. You might even see a group of dragon dancers practicing on a side street.

Then head over to the Golden Gate Bridge for a perfect view of San Francisco. There is even a path on the bridge built just for walkers and people on bikes.

> Chinatown

∨ Golden Gate Bridge

∧ Lombard Street

∨ Icelandic volcano

∨ Strokkur Geyser

< Blue Lagoon

Reykjavík Sights

Does floating in steamy, blue water sound like fun to you? If it does, make sure to visit the Blue Lagoon near the city. If you like sunshine, visit Reykjavík in the summer. At this time of the year, Iceland gets 21 hours of daylight each day.

Geysers (GY-zurz) are located all over Iceland. They may have a funny name, but these springs can shoot hot water more than 100 feet in the air. And if you think that's cool, imagine visiting an actual volcano. Not too far from the city of Reykjavík is a volcano that erupted recently for the first time in about 200 years.

| **Check In** | In what ways are San Francisco and Reykjavík alike and different? |

Discuss

1. What do you think connects the three selections that you read in this book? What makes you think that?

2. In what ways does the surFURS competition show how important the ocean is to one coastal community?

3. Tell why living in the Outer Banks of North Carolina can be fun, and why living there can be challenging.

4. What effect does a bay have on the lives of the people living in San Francisco and Reykjavik?

5. What do you still wonder about life in a coastal community? How can you learn more?